You're invited to be inspired.

Start creating fast, fresh, family-friendly, food, and turn your house into a *home.*

BRISKET 101

Recipes

BEST BRISKETS

SIDES + SLAWS

EXTRAS

LOTS OF LEFTOVERS

BRISKET 101

JAMIE'S 3 GOLDEN RULES FOR PERFECT BRISKET:

1. Rest After You Rub

- At least for 1 hour, ideally for 24 to 36 hours in the refrigerator.

- Seasoning = S+P (50/50 ratio) + Spice Rub, if desired

- The salt is going to penetrate the brisket, season it from the inside out and firm up the meat a little bit. But more importantly, it actually starts tenderizing the meat ahead of the braise and that's particularly useful for hearty/tough cuts like our brisket.

2. Brown Before You Braise

- Brisket benefits enormously from browning the meat before adding aromatic vegetables, a flavorful liquid and some seasonings.

3. Wait 1 Day

- If you can, wait a day to enJOY the fruits of your labor.
  (I confess we are guilty of breaking this golden rule often in my house.)

- Like soup or stew, a brisket generally tastes better a day or so *after* it's made – so all the flavors have the night to marry.

ALL ABOUT AROMATICS

Aromatics are the fun part. This is where you can start to be creative and make a dish your own.

What's an Aromatic?

Aromatics are combinations of vegetables, fruits, spices and herbs that are heated in some fat – like butter, oil, or coconut milk – at the beginning of a dish. The heated fat helps these ingredients release addictive aromas and impart deep flavors into the dish that's being cooked. When you add aromatics to a closed pot suddenly your main ingredient, in this instance our brisket, will slowly start to take on the nuanced flavor of your aromatics. And this is how we start to build layers of flavor, complexity, personality and add that something special to our finished dish.

Basic Brisket Building Block

Start with something from the onion family: red onions, leeks, shallots, scallions.

Time + Brisket = **Best Friends**

Onions + Brisket = **BFF**
There is a simple alchemy between onions and meat, as both sugar and proteins are essential to developing the complex flavors of cooked brisket – making onions and brisket a perfect match.

Personalize Your Aromatics

When you're ready to experiment with your own flavor profiles a good place to start is to consider cuisines you like – think Asian, Italian, Latin and use a combo of veg, fruits, spices, herbs (+ a braising liquid) often used and/or inspired by those cultures and cuisines.

Tip:

Season your aromatics often and season liberally with S + P (very important to building layers of flavor). The salt helps to release the flavors of the veg and starts the mingling of the flavors that is essential to a beautifully complex braised brisket/finished dish.

BUILDING YOUR BRAISING LIQUID AND DEGLAZING

- Traditional braising calls for very little liquid

- If we want to be technical (and nitpicky), when you add more liquid you are stewing the meat—but in the greater cooking world even a brisket, completely covered in liquid, cooked in a pot, with a tight fitting lid, low and slow, is most often called "braising."

- Braising purists may tell you liquid should be no higher than up to ⅓ of the meat. I have heard up to ½ or even up to ⅔ and, like I said, plenty of recipes call for immersing the brisket entirely with liquid. In most of these instances this technique is referred to as braising and will ultimately yield the same tender flavorful result if cooked low and slow. The only difference is that if you have more liquid you will likely need to spend more time reducing it to further concentrate the flavor and thicken it, before serving, if desired.

- Selecting and building a braising liquid: A careful and nice selection of liquids can add layers of flavor to your finished brisket.

  - **Start with:** spirits, alcohol, wine (my favorite go-to!), and beer (Hubby's favorite!) added at the beginning, add depth and richness to a dish that's unmatched.

  - Wine: I love to use dry red or dry white (with poultry). I use a wine I would drink and actually pair/serve with the dish—NOT cooking wine which is full of flavorings and salt (ick!).

  - A nice substitute for alcohol is vinegar. If you don't want to use alcohol, vinegar has some of that sharp acidity you get from alcohol without the alcohol—red wine vinegar, white wine vinegar and apple cider vinegar are all good places to start.

  - Ideally, you want to start your braising liquid by deglazing with wine, beer or vinegar.

What is Deglazing?

- Deglazing refers to dissolving all the wonderful brown caramelized drippings (loaded with flavor!) that are on the bottom of the pan. They are traditionally called sucs (pronounced sooks), from the word *sucre* (sugar) in French.

- To gather the browned bits (called "deglazing") you can add wine, stock or water in a pinch. Especially when deglazing with wine, you want to hear that sizzle—it's going to evaporate most of the alcohol. Whichever deglazing liquid you choose, what's most important is that you dissolve all those cooked-on drippings that we worked so hard to develop from browning the brisket and the aromatics.

- Deglaze over medium heat lightly scraping up the browned bits with a flat-edged wooden spatula or spoon. These tasty little morsels of protein dissolve during the deglazing process and produce a very aromatic fond (foundation) for sauces.

- The next stage is to add something that will impart flavor and volume to your braising liquid:

  - Broth is a very common braising liquid and my second go-to after wine or beer. I like to match broth to protein: a beef broth with beef/brisket, chicken broth with chicken recipes, and so on. There is also vegetable broth on the market. Of the three, chicken is the least assertive so really chicken will pair well with almost any protein. I always have a few boxes of beef, and veg broth in the house and then a larger number of chicken—since it's most versatile—for use at any time.

  - Less common braising liquids that I like to use (in both my braises and marinades) are fruit juices (orange, apple, cranberry, etc...) and the liquid from canned tomatoes, which is another great source of braising liquid.

MARINATING 101

Rules and Regs

The Right Container
Use a shallow, nonreactive dish that will allow marinade to coat the food evenly—even coverage is essential. Most marinades contain an acidic component that helps tenderize the protein. Opt for a nonreactive container, such as a glass or ceramic baking dish. You can also use a large sealable plastic bag; when marinating in the refrigerator, rest the bag on a plate or in a dish in case of leaks. (Heaven forbid!)

How Long?
Arrange the main ingredient in a single layer in the dish. Marinate for at least 30 minutes—at room temperature; if marinating longer, refrigerate. Most briskets can be marinated for up to 24 hours unless otherwise noted in the recipe.

Flip
Flip at least once, halfway through the marinating time, so the liquid covers the brisket evenly.

Room Temp
Let the meat come to room temperature before cooking. (A four-pound brisket will take about one hour.)

Dry and Season
Pat brisket dry before searing for best results. To accentuate the flavor, season the marinated meat with salt and pepper just before cooking.

Watch Carefully

Marinades that contain sugar char quickly when exposed to high heat. To prevent burning, watch carefully when searing.

How to Build a Marinade

Oil (Or Other Fat)

Oil coats meat and becomes infused with all of the flavors in your marinade.

Acid (Like Vinegar or Lemon Juice)

Acid helps tenderize the meat and balance its natural richness.

Something Salty, Something Sweet

Season your marinade with more than salt and white sugar. Try soy sauce, Worcestershire, mustard, fruit juice, or honey.

Herbs, Onions, Garlic

The traditional aromatics will add freshness and depth to your marinade.

Heat Before You Eat

Don't underestimate the power of a little heat to balance a marinade—cayenne, chili, red pepper flakes, hot paprika—add a pinch or more to taste.

SLOW COOKING

- Just like braising, the low, slow gentle heat of a slow cooker is perfect for breaking down collagen into gelatin and softening tough cuts of meat like brisket.

- Obviously, check the owner's manual for details on your slow cooker, but a slow cooker by definition should not reach above 210°F.

- The difference between the high and low settings is how long it takes to reach 210°F, but then on both settings once it reaches the desired/max temp it will hold there.

- The general rule of thumb for brisket is two hours per pound on low in a slow cooker. Hence the set-it-and-forget-it in the morning, for dinner, kinda meal. (Also helpful if your oven is otherwise preoccupied cooking up a holiday storm.)

- Because the heat takes a long time to build up in the slow cooker, and the steam that forms not only aids in the cooking process but also allows a vacuum to form under the lid, I don't recommend lifting the lid to check on the cooking process. Every time the lid is lifted you need to add an additional 20 minutes for the slow cooker to come back to the ideal cooking temp.

TOP TIPS FOR USING YOUR SLOW COOKER

You can prepare great food in your slow cooker without a lot of fuss. Use these tips for preparation and to get the most from your slow cooker to make convenient and delicious meals.

- Brisket Golden Rule #1 also applies to slow cooking: Brown Before you Braise/Slow Cook. Although doing so may add a few extra minutes to your prep, food takes on a whole different look and flavor when browned first.

- Don't overdo the liquid. Very little evaporation occurs in a slow cooker compared to stovetop or oven cooking. Most slow cooker recipes, with the exception of soups and sauces, call for 50 percent less liquid than conventional ones.

- Always cook covered. To maintain the proper balance between time and temperature, always cook with the cover on. If you must peek or stir, do so quickly; it can take up to 20 minutes to recover lost heat after the cover is removed. (Yes, I am repeating myself, but some things are worth repeating.)

- Season liberally. Because slow cooker food cooks longer than other conventional methods, the flavor of herbs and spices can diminish. Fresh herbs should be added during the last 60 minutes of cooking. Also add a pinch or two more of dried herbs than you think necessary. Season to taste with salt and freshly ground black pepper. Taste again and adjust seasoning as needed before serving.

- Don't subject the ceramic cooking container or glass lid to extreme temperatures. The ceramic cooking container and glass cover react to changes in temperature and can crack or break if cold ingredients are added when hot, or if placed on a cold surface when hot. (IT HAPPENED TO ME! When testing these recipes!)

- Do not overfill or underfill. For best cooking results, fill your slow cooker at least halfway and no more than two-thirds.

HOW TO MAKE YOUR OWN SPICE RUB

To make a robust, well-rounded rub be sure all the usual suspects are present and accounted for:

- Heat
- Spice
- Color

For a basic rub, start with salt and sugar for flavor, balance and caramelization, and build by adding:

- Heat: black, white or cayenne pepper
- Smokiness: cumin or chipotle powder
- Personality: herbs or spices to match the meat
- Color: paprika or a mild chili powder

But have fun and PLAY PLAY PLAY!
Add or swap some of these herbs and spices to create your signature rub:

- Allspice
- Cardamom
- Chili Chipotle/Ancho etc…
- Cloves
- Cocoa
- Coffee
- Coriander
- Dried Lemon/Lime Zest
- Dried Minced Garlic/Garlic Powder
- Dried Minced Onion/Onion Powder
- Dried Mustard
- Ground Ginger
- Lemon Pepper
- Oregano
- Parsley
- Rosemary
- Sage
- Sugar Raw/Brown/White
- Thyme
- Turmeric
- And more!

Tip:

Double, triple or quadruple your spice rub and store it in a sealed container with the rest of your spices, it will last just as long.

Here it is. The reason you picked up this book in the first place. **Brisket.** And not just any old recipe. These are **my family's favorites.** From my it-cooks-while-you-sleep brisket to my perfect for any holiday brisket, the gang's all here.

classic
COMFORTING

(Perfect) Classic Oven Braised Brisket

8 to 10 servings

Make this brisket first. The classic flavor profile and techniques employed here will produce the most absolutely (Perfect) Classic Oven Braised Brisket. We are stovetop searing, oven braising, and employing the classic combo of aromatics - onions, carrots, and celery, called a mirepoix in French. (FYI: The classic ratio is 2:1:1 = 2 parts onion to 1 part each carrots and celery—but note it's more than OK to deviate from this ratio based on what you have around—it's the flavor combo that's so tradish and delish.)

Through this recipe you will learn how to deglaze with good-quality dry red wine, enhance and bulk your braising liquid with beef broth, and reduce your sauce to the taste and consistency you like best. Once you master this dish, this flavor profile and these techniques, the sky is the limit when it comes to riffing on this classic or totally inventing your own recipe. But please do not misinterpret classic as boring. This brisket is utter perfection, a family favorite, and beautifully dressed up when surrounded by Cumin Roasted Lemon Carrots (pg. 60) and topped with Crispy Shallots (pg. 100). In fact, this finished dish is simply irresistible.

Ingredients

1 (4–5 pound) beef brisket, 2nd cut
Kosher salt
Freshly cracked pepper
Olive oil
2 medium red onions, sliced
2 medium carrots, diced
2 celery ribs, diced

1 head garlic, minced
3 tablespoons tomato paste
2 cups good-quality dry red wine
1 cup beef broth
1 bouquet garni: 6 parsley stems (or 2 teaspoons dried parsley), 3 thyme sprigs (or 1 teaspoon dried thyme), 3 rosemary sprigs (or 1 teaspoon dried rosemary), 2 bay leaves, 4–6 inch strip of lemon zest, tied in a cheese cloth)

Directions

1. Preheat oven to 300°F.

2. Heat a large Dutch oven, lightly coated with olive oil, over medium-high heat. Pat dry the brisket and generously season both sides with salt and pepper.

3. Sear the brisket, in the hot oil, until nicely browned and caramelized, about 5 minutes per side.

4. Transfer the brisket to a rimmed baking pan and set aside.

5. Add oil if necessary to lightly coat the bottom of the Dutch oven. Add onions, carrots and celery, season with salt and pepper, and sauté stirring occasionally for 10 minutes until the onions are softened and golden. Add garlic and sauté for 1 minute until fragrant. Add the tomato paste, and sear the paste until it has darkened and is very fragrant. The paste should be dark red and not black.

6. Add wine and scrape up any browned bits with a spatula. Add the beef broth.

7. Add brisket and any accumulated juices and the bouquet garni. Cover and braise at 300°F for 3½ to 4 hours or until a fork can be inserted into and removed from the center of the brisket with no resistance.

8. Carefully remove brisket to a cutting board and let rest for 20 minutes. Cover loosely with foil if you will be serving immediately.

9. Strain vegetables and bouquet garni and discard. Pour the braising liquid into a saucepan and reduce over medium heat to concentrate the flavors and/or until the liquid coats the back of a spoon. Skim any fat that pools at the top, if desired. Adjust seasoning once you have reached desired consistency.

10. Slice brisket against the grain and arrange on a platter. Drizzle with sauce and serve any extra sauce in a gravy boat on the side.

Garlic Honey Slow Cooker Brisket

8 servings

This holiday favorite brisket is perfect for Rosh Hashanah with its sweet honey marinade. Of course this recipe can easily be cooked (any time of year) in the oven but using a slow cooker includes the obvious "set it and forget it" benefits as well ensuring your big brisket doesn't commandeer all that valuable oven real estate—especially helpful when whipping up BIG festive holiday meals. As a general rule of thumb, slow cooker math, for brisket, is basically two hours per pound, on low.

You can of course strain and even reduce the sauce before serving, if desired, but note that it's plenty pungent and flavorful as is and serving it with the onions lends a rich body and creamy texture to the final dish (and it's how Hubby and I enJOY this sauce). You really can't go wrong either way. Check out my Careful "Crock Pot" Cooking Tip on pg. 31.

Ingredients

For Marinade
¼ cup olive oil
1 cup honey
½ cup Dijon style mustard
1 head garlic, minced
¼ cup freshly squeezed orange juice
¼ cup freshly squeezed lemon juice
½ teaspoon red chili flakes
½ teaspoon dried thyme

For Brisket
Kosher salt
Freshly cracked black pepper
1 (4-pound) beef brisket, 2nd cut
Olive oil
8 medium onions, peeled and thickly sliced

Directions

1. Combine olive oil, honey, mustard, garlic, orange juice, lemon juice, chili flakes, and thyme in a medium bowl, whisking to blend well. Season brisket with salt and pepper and place in a sealable plastic bag. Add the marinade, seal, and refrigerate at least 1 hour or up to 24 hours, flipping at least once halfway through.

2. Allow brisket to come to room temperature for 1 hour.

3. Spray the insert of a slow cooker with cooking spray.

4. Heat a sauté pan, large enough to hold the brisket, over medium heat. Lightly coat the bottom of the pan with olive oil. Add onions (in batches if necessary), season with salt and pepper, and sauté until just golden, stirring occasionally, about 10 minutes. Transfer to slow cooker insert.

sweet
TENDER

5. Add more oil to the pan as needed to lightly coat. Remove brisket from marinade (reserve marinade), pat dry, and season both sides with salt and pepper.

6. Sear the brisket, in the hot oil, until nicely browned and caramelized, about 5 minutes per side. Transfer to slow cooker insert with pan drippings, scraping up all the browned bits from the bottom of the pan.

7. Pour remaining marinade from plastic bag over brisket and onions, cover, and cook on low for 8 hours or until a fork can be inserted into and removed from the center of the brisket with no resistance.

8. Carefully remove brisket to a cutting board and let rest for 20 minutes. Cover loosely with foil if you will be serving immediately.

9. Bring braising liquid to a gentle simmer in a saucepan to keep warm. Reduce and skim fat as desired. Adjust seasoning once you have reached desired consistency.

10. Slice brisket against the grain and arrange on a platter. Drizzle with sauce and serve any extra sauce in a gravy boat on the side.

 **Recipe adapted from the** JOY of KOSHER Cookbook **by Jamie Geller (William Morrow/HarperCollins 2013).** Order your copy now **for 199 more fast, fresh, family recipes.**

soft
SUCCULENT

Spice Rubbed Oven Seared Brisket

8 servings

This is the 3rd technique for braised brisket. The 36-hour, spice rubbed, oven seared, soft, buttery, brisket is by far the most hands-off of my recipes. I suggest serving it with BBQ sauce, on the side, for dipping, just in case you have an insatiable need for sauce-y brisket. But just so we are clear, the BBQ sauce never gets used at my table—'cause this brisket is that goooood!

As an aside, once you follow Golden Rule #1: Rest After you Rub, you will never make brisket any other way again. The 24- to 36-hour chill-lax time in the fridge (whether with a spice rub or just S + P) tenderizes the meat to a toothsome, luscious, succulent, buttery, consistency like you've never known before.

Ingredients

For Rub
1 tablespoon dried chopped onion or onion powder
1 tablespoon dried chopped garlic or garlic powder
1 tablespoon (sweet, hot or smoked) paprika
1 tablespoon demerara sugar or brown sugar
1 teaspoon ground ginger
1 teaspoon dry mustard
1 teaspoon cumin
1 teaspoon cayenne (or to taste)
Kosher salt
Freshly cracked black pepper

For Brisket
Kosher salt
Freshly cracked black pepper
4-pound beef brisket, 2nd cut
Olive oil
8 medium onions, peeled and thickly sliced

Directions

1. In a small bowl, mix together onion, garlic, paprika, sugar, ginger, mustard, cumin and cayenne.

2. Place brisket on a rimmed baking sheet, pat dry with paper towels, and generously season both sides with salt and pepper. Pat rub onto the brisket on all surfaces. Refrigerate uncovered (or loosely covered with plastic wrap) for 24 to 36 hours.

3. Preheat oven to 350°F. Allow brisket to come to room temperature for 1 hour. Lightly coat

the bottom of a Dutch oven or baking dish (large enough to hold the brisket and onions) with olive oil. Add onions and season with salt and pepper. Place brisket on top of onions.

4. Roast uncovered at 350°F for 30 minutes on each side. Lower the oven temperature to 300°F. Cover the brisket and continue cooking at 300°F for about 3 hours or until a fork can be inserted into and removed from the center of the brisket with no resistance.

5. Carefully remove brisket to a cutting board and let rest for 20 minutes. Cover loosely with foil if you will be serving immediately.

6. Slice brisket against the grain and arrange on a platter. Serve with onions, pan juices and Texas Style BBQ Sauce on the side, if desired.

PHOTOGRAPHY COURTESY OF **DROR HOFFMAN**

Mexi-Style Brisket

8 servings

I love this twist on traditional brisket; the spice rub is so flavorful. I like pairing this Mexican inspired brisket with corn salsa and stuffed poblano peppers. Serve it up at your next fiesta or for Wednesday night din din.

Ingredients

2 tablespoons turbinado (Sugar in the Raw) or dark brown sugar, packed
2 tablespoons dry mustard
1 tablespoon dried chopped garlic or garlic powder
1 tablespoon ground cumin
1 tablespoon dried coriander
1 teaspoon ancho chili powder
1 (4 to 5 pound) beef brisket, 2nd cut
Kosher salt
Freshly cracked black pepper
2 tablespoons olive oil
1 cup beef broth

Directions

1. In a small bowl, mix together sugar, mustard, garlic, cumin, coriander, and chili powder.

2. Place brisket on a rimmed baking sheet, pat dry with paper towels and generously season both sides with salt and pepper. Pat rub onto the brisket on all surfaces. Refrigerate uncovered (or loosely covered with plastic wrap) for 24 to 36 hours.

3. Preheat oven to 300°F. Allow brisket to come to room temperature for 1 hour.

4. Heat a large Dutch oven, lightly coated with olive oil, over medium-high heat.

5. Sear the brisket, in the hot oil, until nicely browned and caramelized, about 5 minutes per side.

6. Add broth. Cover and braise at 300°F for 3½ to 4 hours or until a fork can be inserted into and removed from the center of the brisket with no resistance.

7. Carefully remove brisket to a cutting board and let rest for 20 minutes. Cover loosely with foil if you will be serving immediately.

8. Bring braising liquid to a gentle simmer to keep warm. Reduce and skim fat as desired. Adjust seasoning once you have reached desired consistency.

9. Slice brisket against the grain and arrange on a platter. Drizzle with sauce and serve any extra sauce in a gravy boat on the side.

Recipe adapted from QUICK & KOSHER Meals in Minutes **by Jamie Geller (Feldheim 2010).** Order your copy now **for more than one hundred 20-, 40- and 60- minute meals.**

rich
EARTHY

Beer Braised Slow Cooker Brisket

8 servings

This beer braised brisket is made easy in the slow cooker. Add 1 to 2 cups beef broth for added depth of flavor. Cooking with Beer Tip: For this recipe I recommend ale or stout (ale has fruity, earthy flavors and a bright crispness whereas stout has warmer, toasty, coffee-and-chocolate flavors). But just like I always say—cook with your favorite wine, something you would pair the dish with—you should cook only with your favorite beer. Never cook with a beer you wouldn't drink. Chances are if you don't like the flavor in a mug you won't like it on your plate.

Careful "Crock Pot" Cooking Tip: As discussed the general rule of thumb for slow cooker brisket is two hours per pound, on low. That is assuming your slow cooker does not rise above 210°F. If you know your slow cooker runs on the hot side then check your brisket two hours shy of the expected cooking time. Generally you get penalized for checking by having to add an extra 20 minutes to the total cook time (for each lift-of-the-lid/peek-into-your-pot episode), but this concern is less important if you know your slow cooker runs on the hot side.

Ingredients

- 1 tablespoon (sweet, hot or smoked) paprika
- 3 tablespoons turbinado (Sugar in the Raw) or dark brown sugar, packed
- 1 tablespoon ground cumin
- 1 tablespoon instant coffee granules
- ½ teaspoon dried minced onion or onion powder
- ½ teaspoon dried minced garlic or garlic powder

- 1 (4-pound) beef brisket, 2nd cut
- Kosher salt
- Freshly cracked black pepper
- 2 tablespoons olive oil
- 24-ounce ale or stout
- 1 to 2 cups beef broth, optional

Directions

1. In a small bowl, mix together paprika, sugar, cumin, coffee, onion and garlic.

2. Place brisket on a rimmed baking sheet, pat dry with paper towels and generously season both sides with salt and pepper. Pat rub onto the brisket on all surfaces. Refrigerate uncovered (or loosely covered with plastic wrap) for 24 to 36 hours.

3. Allow brisket to come to room temperature for 1 hour.

4. Spray the insert of a slow cooker with cooking spray.

5. Heat a large Dutch oven, lightly coated with olive oil, over medium-high heat.

6. Sear the brisket, in the hot oil, until nicely browned and caramelized, about 5 minutes per side.

7. Transfer to slow cooker insert with pan drippings, scraping up all the browned bits from the bottom of the pan.

8. Pour beer and broth, if using, over brisket, cover and cook on low for 8 hours or until a fork can be inserted into and removed from the center of the brisket with no resistance.

9. Carefully remove brisket to a cutting board and let rest for 20 minutes. Cover loosely with foil if you will be serving immediately.

10. Pour the braising liquid into a saucepan and reduce over medium heat to concentrate the flavors until the liquid coats the back of a spoon. Skim any fat that pools at the top, if desired. Adjust seasoning once you have reached desired consistency.

11. Slice brisket against the grain and arrange on a platter. Drizzle with sauce and serve any extra sauce in a gravy boat on the side.

classic
REINVENTED

Sweet & Sour Cabbage Brisket

8 servings

One of my most beloved holiday recipes is the Un-Stuffed Cabbage Soup from my first book, QUICK & KOSHER Recipes From The Bride Who Knew Nothing (that's me!). One year for the holidays, I was inspired to turn this family, friend, and neighborhood favorite into an entrée – thankfully it continued to please the palates of all who partook.

Ingredients

1 (4-pound) beef brisket, 2nd cut
Kosher salt
Freshly ground black pepper
1 cup packed turbinado (Sugar in the Raw) or dark brown sugar, divided
1 large onion, thinly sliced
1 (16-ounce) bag shredded cabbage
1 pound baby carrots
1 (14.5-ounce) can crushed tomatoes
Juice of 1 large lemon, about 4 tablespoons
2 tablespoons white wine vinegar
1 cup tomato paste

Directions

1. Place brisket on a rimmed baking sheet, pat dry with paper towels and generously season both sides with salt, pepper and ⅔ cup sugar. Refrigerate uncovered (or loosely covered with plastic wrap) for 24 to 36 hours.

2. Preheat oven to 300°F. Allow brisket to come to room temperature for 1 hour.

3. Heat a large Dutch oven, lightly coated with olive oil, over medium-high heat.

4. Sear the brisket, in the hot oil, until nicely browned and caramelized, about 5 minutes per side. Transfer the brisket to the rimmed baking sheet and set aside.

5. Add oil if necessary to lightly coat the bottom of the Dutch oven. Add onions, cabbage and carrots, season with salt and pepper, and sauté stirring occasionally until the onions are softened and golden about 10 minutes.

6. Add crushed tomatoes with their liquid and scrape up any browned bits with a spatula. Add

lemon juice, vinegar, and remaining ⅓ cup sugar. Mix to combine and bring to a boil. Turn off the heat and add the brisket and any accumulated juices. Spread the tomato paste over the brisket as if you are icing a cake. Cover and braise at 300°F for 3½ to 4 hours or until a fork can be inserted into and removed from the center of the brisket with no resistance.

7. Carefully remove brisket to a cutting board and rest for 20 minutes. Cover loosely with foil if you will be serving immediately.

8. Gently simmer sauce and vegetables to keep warm. Skim fat as desired and adjust for seasoning.

9. Slice brisket against the grain and arrange on a platter with vegetables and sauce.

family
FAVORITE

Brisket in Wine Sauce

8 servings

This rich flavorful brisket is a classic from my first book—it's my go-to for crowds with kids when I'm shortest on time. So you'll notice that Golden Rule #1: Rest After You Rub (at least for one hour, ideally for 24 to 36 hours) is conspicuously missing from the directions below. 'Cause when I'm short on time I do take shortcuts. This recipe doesn't require much slicing or dicing and I always have all the ingredients handy. So, I shared it here without the overnight chill so you don't feel guilty about skipping that step when you're in a rush too. (And because I really wanted you to know that I'm not a crazy stickler for rules.)

As with the Garlic Honey Slow Cooker Brisket, I prefer to serve this dish with the onions. They lend such a creamy texture and silky mouthfeel to the finished dish. (We've spoke about how brisket loves time and brisket loves onions; well, brisket also loves ketchup! You'll find even the poshest of chefs and most seasoned home cooks have a brisket with ketchup recipe... so why should I be left out?)

Ingredients

    1 (4-pound) beef brisket, 2nd cut
    Kosher salt
    Freshly cracked black pepper
    2 tablespoons paprika
    1 teaspoon basil
    4 large onions, sliced
    4 cloves garlic, peeled, smashed
    1 cup dry red wine
    1 cup ketchup
    1 cup beef broth or water

Directions

1. Preheat oven to 300°F.

2. Heat a large Dutch oven, lightly coated with olive oil, over medium-high heat. Pat dry the brisket and generously season both sides with salt, pepper, paprika and basil.

3. Sear the brisket, in the hot oil, until nicely browned and caramelized, about 5 minutes per side. Transfer the brisket to a rimmed baking pan and set aside.

4. Add oil if necessary to lightly coat the bottom of the Dutch oven. Add onions, season with salt and pepper and sauté stirring occasionally until softened and golden about 10 minutes. Add garlic and sauté 1 minute until fragrant about.

5. Add wine and scrape up any browned bits with a spatula. Add ketchup and beef broth, stir to combine.

6. Add brisket and any accumulated juices. Cover and braise at 300°F for 3½ to 4 hours or until a fork can be inserted into and removed from the center of the brisket with no resistance.

7. Carefully remove brisket to a cutting board and let rest for 20 minutes. Cover loosely with foil if you will be serving immediately.

8. Bring braising liquid to a gentle simmer to keep warm. Reduce and skim fat as desired. Adjust seasoning once you have reached desired consistency.

9. Slice brisket against the grain and arrange on a platter. Drizzle with sauce and serve any extra sauce in a gravy boat on the side.

 **Recipe courtesy of** QUICK & KOSHER Recipes From The Bride Who Knew Nothing **by Jamie Geller (Feldheim 2007), the only cookbook that wants to get you out of the kitchen!** Order your copy now.

Spiced Rubbed Brisket with Summer Fruit Salsa

8 servings

This refreshing summer fruit salsa is best when watermelon and blueberries are at their peak. It's an unexpected way to brighten a brisket. During the winter months I turn this into a persimmon tomato salsa and it's equally divine.

Ingredients

For Brisket

2 tablespoons dried chopped onion or onion powder

1 teaspoon dried thyme leaves

2 teaspoons ground allspice

1 teaspoon ground cinnamon

½ teaspoon cayenne pepper, or to taste

1 (4-pound) beef brisket, 2nd cut

Kosher salt

Freshly ground black pepper

8 medium onions, peeled and thickly sliced

For Fruit Salsa

2 cups cubed fresh mango

1 cup fresh blueberries, rinsed and dried

1 cup cubed, seeded watermelon

1 large red onion, finely diced

1 jalapeño, seeded and finely diced

1 large tomato, cubed

⅓ cup finely chopped fresh cilantro

1 tablespoon kosher salt, or to taste

Freshly squeezed juice of 2 limes, about 4 tablespoons

Directions

1. In a small bowl, mix together onion, thyme, allspice, cinnamon and cayenne.

2. Place brisket on a rimmed baking sheet, pat dry with paper towels and generously season both sides with salt and pepper. Pat rub onto the brisket on all surfaces. Refrigerate uncovered (or loosely covered with plastic wrap) for 24 to 36 hours.

3. Preheat oven to 350°F. Allow brisket to come to room temperature for 1 hour. Lightly coat the bottom of a Dutch oven or baking dish (large enough to hold the brisket and onions) with olive oil. Add onions and season with salt and pepper. Place brisket on top of onions.

4. Roast uncovered at 350°F for 30 minutes on each side. Lower the oven temperature to 300°F.

5. Cover the brisket and continue cooking at 300°F for 3 hours or until a fork can be inserted into and removed from the center of the brisket with no resistance.

6. Carefully remove brisket to a cutting board and let rest for 20 minutes. Cover loosely with foil if you will be serving immediately.

7. Prepare the salsa just before serving: Combine mangoes, blueberries, watermelon, onions, jalapeños, tomatoes, cilantro, and lime juice together in a bowl. Season to taste with salt and serve immediately.

8. Slice brisket against the grain and arrange on a platter. Serve with onions, pan juices and Summer Fruit Salsa.

perfectly
SPICED

sweet
TART

Pomegranate Braised Brisket

8 servings

Cranberry juice can easily sub for pomegranate juice as a great braising liquid for this sweet (and ever so slightly tart) holiday brisket.

This recipe calls for flipping the brisket halfway through the braise. While not necessary it's a really nice way to evenly cook the brisket and allow you to check the level of your braising liquid. When I can (as in have time and remember) I do take this extra step, but not always. So no pressure, no guilt trip—just a friendly suggestion to add "the flip" to your brisket repertoire.

Note: You can make a bouquet garni for the thyme and bay leaves so you can easily fish them out before reducing your sauce.

Ingredients

1 (4-pound) beef brisket, 2nd cut
Kosher salt
Freshly ground black pepper
4 tablespoons olive oil, divided
3 medium onions, peeled and cut into eighths
6 cloves garlic, smashed
2 cups pomegranate juice
2 cups chicken broth
3 tablespoons honey
3 bay leaves
1 small bunch fresh thyme (12 sprigs) or 2 teaspoons dried thyme

Directions

1. Place brisket on a rimmed baking sheet, pat dry with paper towels and generously season both sides with salt and pepper. Refrigerate uncovered (or loosely covered with plastic wrap) for 24 to 36 hours.

2. Preheat oven to 300°F. Allow brisket to come to room temperature for 1 hour.

3. Heat a large Dutch oven, lightly coated with olive oil, over medium-high heat.

4. Sear the brisket, in the hot oil, until nicely browned and caramelized, about 5 minutes per side. Transfer the brisket to the rimmed baking sheet and set aside.

5. Add oil if necessary to lightly coat the bottom of the Dutch oven. Add onions, season with salt and pepper, and sauté stirring occasionally until softened and golden about 10 minutes. Add garlic and sauté until fragrant about 1 minute.

6. Add pomegranate juice and scrape up any browned bits with a spatula. Add the broth, honey, bay leaves, and thyme and stir to combine. Bring to a boil, then reduce to a simmer. Add brisket and any accumulated juices. Cover and braise at 300°F for 3½ to 4 hours, flipping halfway through, or until a fork can be inserted into and removed from the center of the brisket with no resistance.

7. Carefully remove brisket to a cutting board and let rest for 20 minutes. Cover loosely with foil if you will be serving immediately.

8. Strain the braising liquid or simply fish out the bay leaves and thyme. Bring braising liquid to a gentle simmer to keep warm. Reduce and skim fat as desired. Adjust seasoning once you have reached desired consistency.

9. Slice brisket against the grain and arrange on a platter. Drizzle with sauce and serve any extra sauce in a gravy boat on the side.

easy
FLAVORFUL

Overnight Brisket

10 servings

It's 8 am and dinner is ready! Oh poor you, you worked so hard! NAH . . . you slept like a baby knowing that dinner was cooking itself while you slumbered.

Low oven temp and a long slow cook session ensures that this brisket is tender and not dried out. Be sure to use a whole brisket with fat on it, or a second-cut brisket (also known as the deckel). This will guarantee a moist, juicy, and savory end result. A first cut brisket will just be stringy.

Ingredients

3 large onions, thinly sliced
3 whole heads of garlic, sliced in half to reveal the cloves
1 whole brisket (fat on) or 2 second cut briskets, such as Grow and Behold brisket
Kosher salt
Freshly cracked black pepper
1 cup dry red wine
3 cups beef or chicken broth
1 cup crushed tomatoes (optional)

Directions

1. Preheat oven to 225°F.

2. Layer sliced onions and garlic in a large roasting pan or Dutch oven. Season brisket with salt and pepper.

3. Place brisket on top of onions and garlic. Pour red wine, broth and tomatoes, if using, into pan. Cover food directly with a layer of parchment (foil will leach onto your food) and then seal tightly with foil.

4. Roast at 225°F for 10 hours.

5. Gently transfer brisket to a cutting board to cool before slicing. While brisket is cooling, strain onions and garlic from pan juices, being sure to press out all juices. Skim fat off pan juices and reduce pan juices on stove top until it coats the back of a spoon.

6. Slice brisket across the grain and transfer back to braising pan. Store in refrigerator for up to 3 days or freeze for 1 month (freeze reduced braising liquid separately).

7. Reheat brisket, covered in a low oven at 250°F until hot. Serve with reduced pan juices.

Roasted Apple Brisket

8 servings

Since the custom of eating apples on Rosh Hashanah revives our memory of Biblical blessings, let's combine it with a more recent, beloved tradition. Nu, what's a Yuntif without brisket?

Ingredients

2½-pound brisket
3 tablespoons brown sugar
1 teaspoon kosher salt
Freshly ground black pepper
2 tablespoons extra virgin olive oil
3 medium gala apples, cored and cut into wedges
1 small bunch fresh thyme, or 2 teaspoons dried thyme
2 cups apple juice

Directions

1. Preheat oven to 375°F.

2. Season both sides of brisket with sugar, salt, and pepper. Heat evoo in a large Dutch oven over medium-high heat. Add brisket and brown 5 minutes on each side. Remove from the pan and set aside.

3. Add apples to the pan, and cook 5 minutes or until nicely browned. Stir in thyme, and return brisket to the pan.

4. Add apple juice, cover, and bake at 375°F for 1½ to 2 hours, or until tender.

5. Remove brisket and apples from the Dutch oven and let rest.

6. Transfer the pan to the stove and bring liquid to a boil over medium. Simmer for 15 minutes or until reduced by half. Pour into a gravy boat or serving bowl.

7. Slice brisket into ¼-inch thick slices and place on a serving platter. Place cooked apples around brisket and serve with sauce on the side.

taste of
TRADITION

Braised Brisket with Dates and Red Wine

10 servings

Naturally sweet and caramel-flavored dates paired with wine, onions and garlic make this brisket extra special and over the top delicious.

Feel free to add fresh or dried herbs like thyme and rosemary to the braising liquid. These herbs will balance the sweetness and bring out flavor notes in the wine. Dried ancho chilies add earthiness and deep bass notes to round out this holiday brisket.

Ingredients

Extra virgin olive oil
12-14 pound whole brisket (whole brisket will yield a meltingly tender brisket)
2 large Spanish onions, sliced
1 bottle dry red wine (Cabernet Sauvignon, Merlot, Pinot Noir)
2 whole heads garlic, sliced in half crosswise to expose the cloves
2 cups chicken broth
¼ cup tomato paste
2 cups chopped pitted dates
Kosher salt
Freshly cracked black pepper

Directions

1. Preheat oven to 320°F.

2. Pat dry brisket. (Wet brisket will not caramelize, it will just steam!) Season brisket with salt and pepper. Heat a braising pan or large Dutch oven, lightly coated with evoo over medium high heat. If you don't have a pan large enough to accommodate the whole piece of meat, cut the meat in half and sear each piece separately—do not be afraid to cut it in half.

3. Sear the brisket for 5 to 7 minutes per side, on both sides being sure to allow each side to caramelize and turn dark brown. Remove brisket and set aside.

4. Add onions to the pan and caramelize being sure to season with salt and pepper, until dark brown and very soft, 10 to 15 minutes.

5. Pour in the bottle of wine, then add 2 heads garlic, 2 cups chicken broth, and tomato paste.

6. Nestle brisket back into the pan. Add dates, cover and place in oven.

7. Braise brisket for 3½ to 4 hours or until a fork can be inserted easily without resistance.

8. Remove brisket and allow to cool before slicing across the grain.

9. Taste and adjust seasoning of the braising liquid, strain if desired, serve over brisket until reduced by half. Pour into a gravy boat or serving bowl.

10. Slice brisket into ¼-inch thick slices and place on a serving platter. Place cooked apples around brisket and serve with sauce on the side.

extra
SPECIAL

Oven Seared Silan Brisket

8 servings

This technique for 36-hour, spice-rubbed, oven-seared, soft, buttery brisket is pretty much hands-off. Of course, the secret is my Brisket Golden Rule: Rest After You Rub. The 24- to 36-hour resting time in the fridge (whether with a spice rub or just S+P) tenderizes the meat to a consistency like you've never known before. Silan imparts a richer flavor than regular honey. If you can't find silan, use ¾ cup of regular honey.

Ingredients

For Rub
1 tablespoon dried chopped onion or onion powder
1 tablespoon dried chopped garlic or garlic powder
1 tablespoon (sweet, hot, or smoked) paprika
1 tablespoon demerara or brown sugar
1 teaspoon ground ginger
1 teaspoon dry mustard
1 teaspoon cumin
1 teaspoon cayenne (or to taste)
Kosher salt
Freshly cracked black pepper

For Brisket
Kosher salt
Freshly cracked black pepper
4-pound beef brisket, second cut
Extra virgin olive oil
8 large onions, peeled
　　and thickly sliced
1 cup silan (date honey)
2 cups chicken or beef broth

Directions

1. In a small bowl, mix together onion, garlic, paprika, sugar, ginger, mustard, cumin, and cayenne.

2. Place brisket on a rimmed baking sheet, pat dry with paper towels, and generously season both sides with salt and pepper.

3. Pat rub onto the brisket on all surfaces. Refrigerate, uncovered (or loosely covered with plastic wrap), for 24 to 36 hours.

4. Preheat oven to 350°F.

5. Allow brisket to come to room temperature for 1 hour.

6. Lightly coat the bottom of a Dutch oven or baking dish (large enough to hold the brisket and onions) with oil.

7. Add onions and season with salt and pepper. Place brisket on top of onions.

8. Roast at 350°F, uncovered, for 30 minutes on each side.

9. Pour and brush silan over brisket then, pour over the broth. Lower the oven temperature to 300°F. Cover brisket and continue cooking at 300°F for about 3 hours or until a fork can be inserted into and removed from the center of the brisket with no resistance.

10. Carefully remove brisket to a cutting board and let rest for 20 minutes.

11. Cover loosely with foil if you will be serving immediately.

12. Slice brisket against the grain and arrange on a platter. Serve with onions and pan juices.

40 Best Brisket, Sides, Slaws and Leftover Recipes

luscious
TENDER

vibrant
FRESH

Argentinean Brisket with Chimichurri

8 servings

Originally from Argentina, chimichurri is a popular herb sauce used across Latin cooking. Basic "green" chimichurri is made from parsley, garlic, olive oil, oregano, and white or red vinegar. Tweak the sauce to your liking with some additional flavorings, such as cilantro, paprika, cumin, thyme, and lemon. It's traditionally served with grilled meat, but I also like it with white-fleshed fish or chicken, or by the spoonful. You know me by now, so you can't be surprised.

Ingredients

For Brisket
2 tablespoons paprika
2 tablespoons ground cumin
1 tablespoon kosher salt
1 tablespoon dried oregano
1 tablespoon garlic powder
1 teaspoon cayenne pepper
3½ pound brisket
3 tablespoons canola oil
1 cup beef broth
2 tablespoons red wine vinegar

For Chimichurri
1½ cups chopped fresh flat-leaf parsley
1 tablespoon dried oregano
3 garlic cloves, smashed
Zest and juice of 1 lemon
1 tablespoon red wine vinegar
1 teaspoon kosher salt
½ teaspoon freshly ground black pepper
1 teaspoon red pepper flakes (optional)
½ cup extra virgin olive oil

Directions

1. Preheat the oven to 375°F.

2. In a small bowl, combine the paprika, cumin, salt, oregano, garlic powder, and cayenne; mix well. Rub the mixture all over the meat. Heat the canola oil in a Dutch oven over medium-high heat and sear the meat for 3 to 5 minutes on each side. Add the broth and vinegar, cover, and transfer to the oven. Roast at 375°F for 2 hours until tender.

3. Transfer the brisket to a cutting board and let rest at least 15 minutes before slicing.

4. To make the chimichurri sauce, combine the parsley, oregano, garlic, lemon zest and juice, vinegar, salt, black pepper, and red pepper flakes, if using, in a food processor. Pulse to coarsely chop, stopping to scrape down the sides. With the processor running, slowly add the olive oil in a stream until you have a fairly smooth but still slightly chunky sauce.

5. Slice the brisket ¼-inch thick against the grain, transfer it to a serving plate, and drizzle the chimichurri sauce on top.

I'm letting you in on a little **secret.** Brisket goes with almost **anything.** Kugel, potatoes, slaw, you name it. But I think the **robust flavors** in my recipes pair perfectly with these **special sides.**

Cumin Roasted Lemon Carrots

4 servings

Ingredients

- 2 pounds baby carrots with tops, tops cut off with an inch left attached
- 2 to 3 tablespoons extra-virgin olive oil
- 1 teaspoon cumin
- Kosher salt
- Freshly cracked pepper
- Juice from ½ a small lemon

Directions

1. Preheat oven to 400°F, and line a baking sheet with parchment paper.

2. Toss the carrots with olive oil, cumin, salt and pepper and place in the lined baking pan. Don't overcrowd the carrots or they won't brown evenly.

3. Roast carrots at 400°F for 15 to 20 minutes until they are light, toasty brown but still show their gorgeous color. You should be able to pierce the carrot with a fork and have a little resistance.

4. Brighten with a squeeze of fresh lemon juice just before serving.

Rosemary Roasted Potatoes

8 servings

Ingredients

- 4 pounds mixed fingerling and new potatoes, halved
- 4 tablespoons olive oil
- 3 cloves garlic, smashed
- 3 tablespoons fresh rosemary or 1 tablespoon dried
- Kosher salt
- Freshly ground black pepper

Directions

1. Preheat oven to 400°F. Line 2 large baking pans with parchment paper.

2. Toss the potatoes with oil, garlic, rosemary, salt and pepper and place in the prepared pans.

3. Don't overcrowd the potatoes or they won't brown evenly.

4. Roast at 400°F 30 to 40 minutes until nicely browned and crisp on the outside and tender on the inside.

5. Check for doneness by piercing a few potatoes with a fork—the tines should sink easily into the tender flesh. (Or you could always just taste test—which I've been known to do on an occasion or two!).

REMEMBER WHEN ROASTING

KEEP IT UNIFORM
Keep veg the same size for even cooking.

1:1 RATIO
It's 1 tablespoon oil per 1 pound of veg—if you splurge (and there are plenty of occasions where that is perfectly acceptable) and add a little more oil it will cut down on the total roasting time.

CHECK AND ROTATE
Rotate pan(s) halfway through the cook time.

Wilted Spinach with Garlic Chips

6 servings

Ingredients

8 cloves garlic, peeled and thinly sliced

½ cup olive oil plus 2 tablespoons, divided

3 (6-ounce) bags baby spinach

½ teaspoon kosher salt

Freshly ground black pepper

Directions

Place sliced garlic and olive oil in a small saucepan and bring to a simmer over medium-high heat. Once bubbling reduce to medium low and cook 5 to 8 minutes or until garlic is lightly browned and crispy. Remove garlic with a fork or slotted spoon and place on paper towel to drain.

Heat 2 tablespoons olive oil in a large sauté pan over medium high heat. Add spinach and cook for 2 to 4 minutes, stirring constantly, until wilted and warm. Season with salt and pepper.

Transfer spinach to a serving plate and garnish with crispy garlic slices.

Recipe adapted from the JOY of KOSHER Cookbook by Jamie Geller (William Morrow/HarperCollins 2013). Order your copy now for 199 more fast, fresh, family recipes.

Baked Spicy Sweet Potato Fries

4 servings

Baked not fried, sweet not white, spiced just right—what's not to love about these fries? I serve them at BBQs, for Shabbos, for weeknight suppers—there is simply no gathering that can't be enhanced by these Baked Spicy Sweet Potato Fries.

For a lighter yet still delicious version of this recipe you could omit the oil and instead use baking spray. Once laid out on the baking sheets, lightly spray the fries and then season and bake according to directions.

Ingredients

2 pounds (about 4 large) sweet potatoes, peeled and cut into ⅓-inch thick slices

2 to 4 tablespoons olive oil

1 teaspoon ground cumin

1 teaspoon garlic powder

½ teaspoon cayenne pepper, or to taste

Kosher salt

Freshly ground black pepper

Fresh herbs, for garnish, optional

Ketchup, honey mustard, or BBQ Sauce, for serving, optional

Directions

1. Preheat oven to 425°F. Line 2 large baking pans with parchment paper.

2. Toss the potatoes with oil, cumin, garlic powder, cayenne, salt and pepper and place in the prepared pans. Don't overcrowd the potatoes or they won't brown evenly.

3. Bake at 425°F for 1 hour until nicely browned and crisp on the outside and tender on the inside.

4. Garnish with fresh herbs and serve with ketchup, honey mustard or BBQ on the side, if desired.

Recipe courtesy of QUICK & KOSHER Recipes From The Bride Who Knew Nothing **by Jamie Geller** (Feldheim 2007), the only cookbook that wants to get you out of the kitchen!

Dried Fruit and Challah Stuffing

8 to 10 servings

You can use any leftover bread for this recipe, but I like the health bonus of using whole wheat challah and it adds a nice nutty flavor that compliments the chestnuts* in this dish. Don't save this recipe for Thanksgiving; it is really fabulous any time.

*Some people have the custom to refrain from nuts over the high holidays because the numerical value of the Hebrew letters of the word "nut" are equal to the numerical value of the Hebrew letters of the word "sin"—so simply leave out the chestnuts (no other adjustments needed) if it is in fact your custom and you want to make this over the high holidays.

Ingredients

- 1 tablespoon olive oil
- 1 large onion, chopped
- 4 stalks celery, chopped
- 2 (3.5-ounce) bags roasted chestnuts, halved
- 2 cups assorted dried fruit (such as sour cherries, apricots, cranberries, etc.)
- 4 tablespoons chopped fresh sage or 3 teaspoons dried
- 2 tablespoons chopped fresh parsley or 1 teaspoon dried
- 8 cups (1-inch) cubed challah
- 2 cups chicken broth
- 1 teaspoon kosher salt
- 1 teaspoon freshly ground black pepper

Directions

1. Preheat oven to 400°F. Lightly grease a 2.75-quart baking dish and set aside.

2. Heat olive oil in a large Dutch oven over medium high heat. Sauté onion and celery for 8 to 10 minutes.

3. Add chestnuts, dried fruit, sage and parsley and cook 2 minutes more.

4. Stir in challah, chicken stock, salt and pepper and remove from heat.

5. Transfer stuffing to greased baking dish and cover with foil. Bake 30 minutes. Remove foil and bake 10 minutes more or until lightly browned.

Recipe adapted from the JOY of KOSHER Cookbook **by Jamie Geller (William Morrow/HarperCollins 2013).** Order your copy now **for 199 more fast, fresh, family recipes.**

Warm Potato Salad with Horseradish Sauce

4 servings

This recipe is heaven in a potato salad. Warm, crispy, creamy with a hint of heat – I have never tasted a better potato salad, ever! You will need half a cup of sauce per 2 pounds of potatoes. I like equal parts horseradish sauce and mayo but feel free to play with the ratio to intensify the bite - even add fresh or prepared white horseradish for more of a kick. For the potatoes use a combo of red bliss, fingerling, sweet potatoes or even plain old Russets. You can dice the potatoes before or after boiling. And you can even boil the potatoes a day or two in advance of preparing the salad.

Ingredients

- ¼ cup horseradish sauce
- ¼ cup regular or light mayonnaise
- 2 tablespoons olive oil
- 2 pounds cooked potatoes halved or cut small such as red bliss, fingerling or sweet potatoes
- ¼ cup sliced red onion
- Kosher salt
- Freshly ground black pepper
- Mix of fresh parsley, tarragon, dill, or scallions, chopped, for garnish

Directions

1. In a large mixing bowl place Horseradish Sauce and mayonnaise and mix to combine, set aside.

2. Heat oil in a large heavy bottomed skillet over medium-high to high heat. Once oil starts to shimmer, add potatoes in a single layer. Don't overcrowd the pan or your potatoes won't crisp; if necessary fry in batches.

3. Leave the potatoes alone for a minute. Shake the pan; the potatoes should move freely.

4. Shake the pan every minute or so to keep the potatoes from sticking. After 5 to 7 minutes potatoes will have browned. Flip potatoes and brown on the second side for 5 to 7 minutes more.

5. Add onions the last 2 to 3 minutes.

6. Transfer warm potatoes and onions to the bowl with horseradish sauce. Toss to coat and season to taste with salt and pepper.

7. Serve warm garnished with scallions and fresh herbs of your choice.

Salt and Pepper Noodle Kugel with Roasted Garlic

12 servings

For an elegant presentation twist divide the batter into jumbo muffin tins that have been greased with cooking spray.

Ingredients

Cooking spray

10 cloves garlic, peeled

2 tablespoons olive oil

1 (16-ounce) package fine egg noodles

⅓ cup olive oil

4 eggs

½ teaspoon kosher salt

1 teaspoon freshly ground black pepper

Pinch cayenne pepper, optional

Directions

1. Preheat oven to 250°F. Lightly grease a 9- x 13-inch baking dish.

2. Place garlic in the baking dish in a single layer and drizzle with olive oil. Bake at 250°F for 15 minutes, until garlic is soft.

3. Remove garlic from the oven, mash and set aside. Raise the oven temperature to 350°F.

4. Meanwhile boil egg noodles until just tender. Drain, toss with oil and set aside.

5. In a large bowl, lightly beat eggs with salt, black pepper, and cayenne if desired.

6. Stir in garlic, followed by noodle mixture until well combined.

7. Spoon into prepared pan and bake at 350°F for 1 hour.

Creamy Smashed Potatoes with Chives

6 servings

Chunkier and more rustic than your standard mash, these spuds are enhanced by the color and flavor of fresh chives. For a dairy meal swap the oil for butter and the non-dairy sour cream for dairy sour cream or Greek-style yogurt.

Ingredients

- 3 pounds baby Yukon Gold or fingerling potatoes, cut into ½-inch pieces
- 1 tablespoon kosher salt
- 4 tablespoons olive oil
- 6 tablespoons non-dairy sour cream
- ¼ cup chopped chives
- 1 teaspoon garlic powder
- Kosher salt
- Freshly ground black pepper

Directions

1. Place potatoes in a large pot, cover with water and add salt. Bring to a boil over high heat and reduce to a simmer.

2. Cook potatoes 15 to 20 minutes or until tender. Drain well and return to the pot.

3. Mash with a potato masher, leaving some large pieces.

4. Mix in oil, non-dairy sour cream, chives and chunky garlic powder.

5. Season to taste with salt and pepper.

Hasselback Potatoes with Garlic Parsley Oil

8 large potatoes

This recipe features Garlic Parsley Oil but you can easily personalize your spuds. Try minced red onions, spices, panko crumbs—even shredded cheese with a dairy meal!

Ingredients

8 large potatoes, Yukon Gold, Russet, or Red Bliss
½ cup olive oil plus 1 to 2 teaspoons
Kosher salt
Freshly ground black pepper
2 tablespoons minced parsley
2 tablespoons minced garlic

Directions

1. Heat the oven to 425°F with a rack in the lower-middle position.

2. Scrub the potatoes clean and pat them dry.

3. Cut slits into the potato, stopping just before you cut through so that the slices stay connected at the bottom of the potato. Space the slices ½-inch to ¼-inch apart. You can rest the potato in a large serving spoon and use that as a guide for when to stop slicing—slice straight down and when your knife hits the edge of the spoon, stop slicing.

4. Arrange the potatoes in a baking dish large enough to hold them without overcrowding (so they have room to crisp up and don't steam). Brush the potatoes all over with ¼ cup of olive oil including the bottoms.

5. Sprinkle the potatoes generously with salt and pepper.

6. Bake the potatoes at 425°F for 30 minutes. At this point, the layers will start separating. Remove the pan from the oven and brush the potatoes again with the remaining ¼ cup olive oil—you can nudge the layers apart if they're still sticking together. Make sure some of the oil drips down into the space between the slices.

7. Bake for another 30 to 40 minutes, until the potatoes are crispy on the edges and easily

pierce in the middle with a paring knife. (Total baking time is 60 to 70 minutes for average potatoes; if your potatoes are on the small side or are larger, adjust cooking time accordingly.)

8. To add the garlic parsley oil: mix together 2 tablespoons minced parsley, 2 tablespoons minced garlic and 1 to 2 teaspoons olive oil. Stuff into the slits and brush over the top 5 to 10 minutes before the end of cooking.

9. Serve immediately. These potatoes are best straight from the oven while the edges are at their crispiest.

Poppy Seed Slaw

4 cups coleslaw

Ingredients

- 4 cups shredded green cabbage
- 1 cup shredded carrots
- 8 green onions, chopped, green parts only
- ½ cup light mayonnaise
- 2 tablespoons apple cider vinegar
- 1 tablespoon + 1 teaspoon poppy seeds
- 1 teaspoon kosher salt
- A few sprinkles of sugar, or more to taste

Directions

1. In a medium bowl combine cabbage, carrots, onions, mayonnaise, vinegar, poppy seeds and salt. Stir well to evenly coat and combine.

2. Season to taste with sugar.

3. Refrigerate for at least 15 minutes or up to 24 hours before serving.

4. Serve alongside brisket or as a topping for burgers, hot dogs or grilled chicken.

Tropical Slaw

4 cups coleslaw

Filled with all the usual slaw suspects (plus pineapple, mango and red onion), this Tropical Slaw is a sweet twist on a classic.

Ingredients

- 1 cup shredded green cabbage
- 1 cup shredded red cabbage
- ½ cup shredded carrots
- 1 cup diced pineapple
- 1 ripe mango, diced
- ½ medium red onion, thinly sliced
- 4 tablespoons light mayonnaise
- 2 tablespoons apple cider vinegar
- Juice of 1 lime
- ½ teaspoon kosher salt
- A few sprinkles of sugar, or more to taste

Directions

1. In a medium bowl combine cabbage, carrots, pineapple, mango, red onion, mayonnaise, vinegar, lime juice, and salt. Stir well to evenly coat and combine.

2. Season to taste with sugar. Refrigerate for at least 15 minutes or up to 24 hours before serving.

Creamy Rainbow Slaw

6 cups coleslaw

What I love about my slaw recipes is how deliciously pretty they all are. Pleasing to the palate and easy on the eyes. This rainbow version doesn't disappoint, and with the addition of the peppers it's heartier than your standard slaw.

Variation: Don't have non-dairy cream cheese on hand, or don't care for it? Use non-dairy sour cream instead. Although if you don't care for the pareve cream cheese, I am guessing the sour cream is off your list too. Easy enough, just use 1/2 cup mayo and call it a day. Also try adding half a thinly sliced red onion for a slight bite.

Ingredients

3 cups shredded green cabbage

1 cup shredded red cabbage

1 cup shredded carrots

½ red bell pepper, thinly sliced

½ yellow bell pepper, thinly sliced

½ green bell pepper, thinly sliced

2 tablespoons apple cider vinegar

⅓ cup light mayonnaise

⅓ cup non-dairy cream cheese

2 tablespoons sugar

½ teaspoon kosher salt

½ teaspoon freshly ground black pepper

Directions

1. Combine cabbages, carrots and peppers in a large bowl.

2. Whisk together vinegar, mayonnaise, non-dairy cream cheese, sugar, salt and pepper until creamy.

3. Pour desired amount of dressing over coleslaw mix and toss until well coated.

4. Store any remaining dressing in a sealable container in the refrigerator for up to 2 weeks.

5. Refrigerate coleslaw for at least 15 minutes or up to 24 hours before serving.

Apple, Celery Root and Kohlrabi Slaw

6 Servings

Loosely inspired by the hotel and salad that I love, this reinterpretation of a Waldorf Salad is a crisp, fall slaw incorporating apples, honey and pomegranates.

Making acidulated water is a handy trick when you want to keep fruits and vegetables from browning. Water and usually lemon or lime juice are combined to provide an acidic mixture. Vinegar as well as citric acid (even vitamin C tablets) work as well.

Ingredients

- 1 Granny Smith apple, cut into julienne
- 1 Lady apple, cut into julienne
- 1 medium kohlrabi, peeled and cut into julienne
- 1 small celery root, peeled and cut into julienne
- 2 celery stalks, cut into very thin bias
- 1 lemon, juiced and put into 4 cups water
  to create acidulated water

Directions

1. Place apples, kohlrabi, celery root, and celery into lemon water (acidulated water). (The apples, kohlrabi, celery root and celery may be kept in acidulated water, in refrigerator for up to 1 day before serving.)

2. Whisk mayonnaise, honey, vinegar, salt, and pepper together until smooth. Drain apple mixture and shake off water.

3. Toss apples, kohlrabi, celery root, and celery with vinaigrette. Season with salt and pepper to taste.

4. Garnish with pomegranate arils, parsley leaves, and celery leaves.

5. The finished slaw may be stored, covered, in the refrigerator for up to 6 hours before serving.

Potato Salad with Arugula and Tomato

6 Servings

This is a lighter version of potato salad that I like to make on those super hot days when I just want something cool, refreshing and a little bit healthier.

Ingredients

- 1½ pound small red potatoes, scrubbed and halved
- 4 tablespoon champagne vinegar or white wine vinegar
- 4 tablespoon extra virgin olive oil
- 1 lemon, juiced
- 2 teaspoon kosher salt
- Freshly ground black pepper
- 4 green onions, chopped
- 2 pint cherry tomatoes
- 1 cup arugula

Directions

1. In a medium saucepan, cover potatoes with cold water and bring to a boil. Cook over medium high heat until potatoes are tender, 12 to 16 minutes. Drain well and cool completely.

2. While potatoes are cooking prepare dressing. In a small bowl, whisk together vinegar, oil, lemon juice, salt and pepper and set aside.

3. In a large bowl, combine potatoes with green onions, tomatoes and arugula and toss to combine.

4. Pour dressing over potato salad and toss to evenly coat.

5. Potato salad can be served room temperature or chilled. Can be made 2 days in advance, keeping arugula and dressing separate and combining just before serving.

Sweet Potato Salad with Tahini Dressing

4 to 6 Servings

Everyone in the family will love this updated summer classic. For amped-up flavor and nutrition, we don't peel our sweet potatoes. Leftover potato salad can be stored, covered, in the refrigerator for up to 3 days.

Ingredients

- 3 large sweet potatoes, scrubbed, unpeeled and cut into 2-inch dice
- Extra virgin olive oil
- Kosher salt
- Freshly ground black pepper
- ½ cup tahini
- ½ teaspoon cumin
- 2 garlic cloves, grated on a microplane

Directions

1. Preheat oven to 375°F. Line a baking sheet with parchment paper.

2. Arrange potatoes on lined sheet and drizzle with evoo, salt, and pepper. Roast at 375°F for 40 minutes, stirring occasionally, until tender and browned.

3. Whisk tahini, cumin, and garlic in a small bowl. Toss with potatoes (while still warm so the dressing soaks in—YUM!). Arrange on a platter.

4. Serve warm or cold.

Carrot and Chard Ribbons

8 to 10 Servings

Sweet carrots and savory Swiss chard ribbons, my new favorite side. Kale is an excellent swap for chard in this recipe.

Ingredients

2 pounds carrots, peeled and sliced on an angle ¼-inch thick

8 to 10 large Swiss chard leaves, tough stems and center ribs removed and leaves thinly sliced

2 tablespoons extra virgin olive oil

2 cloves garlic, smashed

1 tablespoon chopped fresh parsley

Kosher salt

Freshly ground black pepper

Directions

1. Bring a large saucepan half-full of water to a boil.

2. Add carrots and cook until barely crisp-tender, about 7 minutes.

3. Drain carrots and return to the pot with chard, oil, garlic, and parsley.

4. Season with salt and pepper.

5. Sauté over medium heat until chard is just wilted.

Za'atar Carrots with Green Carrot Top Tahini

4 Servings

When life gives you carrots and their tops, make this Israeli-inspired side, vegetarian main, or mezze (Mediterranean small plate). No more throwing out your vegetable tops — use them.

Green tahini is all the rage and I love this version for many reasons. Soft carrot tops (the greens—save the tough stems for making vegetable broth) have a delicate carrot flavor and when combined with honey, a splash of lemon, and a bit of garlic, create an addicting sauce you will want to schmear on everything. Ok, maybe not on cake, but for sure on everything else. Don't get hung up on exact measurements here. Just go for the bright green color and flavor.

Ingredients

For Tahini

1 cup chopped carrot greens

½ cup chopped flat-leaf parsley

½ cup fresh mint, basil, or dill

3 garlic cloves

¼ cup fresh lemon juice

1 tablespoon honey

3 tablespoons extra virgin olive oil

1½ cups tahini

Kosher salt

For Za'atar Carrots

1 bunch carrots (colorful carrots are nice here)

2 tablespoons extra virgin olive oil

2 tablespoons za'atar

Kosher salt

Freshly ground black pepper

Garnish: rough chopped carrot tops

Directions

Green Carrot-Top Tahini:

1. Place carrot greens, parsley, mint, garlic, lemon juice, honey, and evoo in food processor. Puree at high speed until a bright green pesto has formed. Add tahini and pulse to mix.

2. Taste the sauce; it probably needs salt! Adjust seasoning. Leftover tahini can be stored covered in the fridge for up to 5 days.

Za'atar Carrots:

1. Preheat oven to 375°F. Line a baking sheet with parchment paper.

2. Cut carrots in half lengthwise and arrange on prepared baking sheet.

3. Drizzle carrots with evoo, za'atar, salt, and pepper. Roast at 375°F for 20 to 30 minutes, stirring occasionally until tender and browned.

4. Schmear a platter with a good dollop of Carrot-Top Tahini and arrange carrots on the sauce. Garnish with a drizzle of evoo and additional chopped carrot tops.

Here are a couple of **extra recipes** you'll want to serve **alongside** your brisket.

Crispy Shallots

Half cup shallots

I learned this genius brisket/pot roast topping from one of my favorites, Chef Laura Frankel. Now my entire family can't have brisket, or burgers, or almost anything (except for maybe ice cream) without Crispy Shallots. They are so good that last week I ate half of them fresh from the fry pan, then my daughter and hubby ate the other half, and then I had none left. So now I know to make at least four batches, one for enjoying solo, immediately, one for all the "pickers" and "tasters" and "testers" roaming around my kitchen and a double batch for dinner.

Tip: Save the tasty oil in the refrigerator (for up to 2 weeks) and use for sautéing, stir frying, drizzling on bread, in dressings, or simply as fabulous finishing oil. YUM!

Ingredients

Olive oil or canola oil
4 large shallots, peeled and sliced very thinly on a mandoline or with a knife
Kosher salt
Freshly cracked pepper

Directions

1. Heat a ½-inch of oil in a large sauté pan over medium-low heat. Add shallots; reduce heat to low and cook, stirring often until they are a rich golden brown. Be patient; this could take 20 to 40 minutes but also watch carefully as shallots can go from gorgeous golden brown to burnt quickly.

2. Remove the shallots from the oil with a slotted spoon, drain well, and spread out to cool, in a single layer, on paper towel lined plates. Season with salt and pepper. Shallots will crisp as they cool.

3. Best served fresh, but once the shallots have dried and crisped, they can be stored, covered, at room temperature (in a cool, dark place) or in the refrigerator for several days.

Texas-Style Barbeque Sauce

2¼ cups barbecue sauce

This recipe was adapted from Aaron Franklin's famous sauce—I figured who better to go to than the King of Texas BBQ!

Ingredients

- ¼ cup olive oil
- 1 small onion, finely minced
- 1½ cups ketchup
- ½ cup apple cider vinegar
- 2 ounces light brown sugar
- 1 teaspoon toasted garlic powder
- 1 teaspoon chili powder (try ancho or chipotle)
- Juice from ½ a large lemon, about 2 tablespoons
- 1 tsp kosher salt
- 1 tsp black pepper

Directions

1. In a 2- or 3-quart saucepan, heat oil over medium-high heat and sauté onions until soft and translucent.

2. Add ketchup, vinegar, sugar, garlic, chili powder, lemon juice, salt, and pepper and bring to a boil; reduce heat and simmer for 30 minutes.

3. Check and adjust seasoning.

4. Serve warm with brisket or barbecue.

You **worked hard** for **all that flavor.** Your brisket **deserves more** than reheat & eat. Here's how to use your **leftover brisket** in some really **fun and delicious ways!**

Brisket Tacos

12 tacos

When I whipped these up in a matter of minutes Hubby was like "that was so quick—you should make these all the time!" They're quick because I'm using leftover brisket and not browning the meat from scratch. This shortcut makes us all happy—both the cook and the family of eaters.

Ingredients

1 pound of leftover brisket

12 hard shell corn tacos or
   soft shell corn tortillas

Garnishes: shredded lettuce, avocado,
   sliced jalapeños, non-dairy sour cream,
   salsa or diced tomatoes, sliced radishes,
   fresh cilantro, lime wedges

Directions

1. Divide brisket among taco shells or tortillas. Top with desired garnishes and serve!

Brisket Stuffed Matzo Balls

16 to 18 matzo balls

My cousin Bracha gave me this recipe for light, fluffy and perfectly round matzo balls when I moved to Israel and asked her where to find matzo ball mix. I will NEVER go back to making matzo balls from a mix again. Apparently everyone agrees with me as this recipe has over 150K views online.

When thinking about brisket leftover ideas and recipes, I came up with brisket wontons, brisket pot stickers, and brisket egg rolls and then thought to myself – why borrow from other cultures before trying Brisket Stuffed Matzo Balls – and so this recipe was born.

Tip: Not simply for chicken soup; I pair matzo balls with everything -- cabbage soup, tomato soup, vegetable soup, split pea soup. I don't initially cook the matzo balls in the soup (especially clear broths) as that can cause the soup to become cloudy. Instead, once the matzo balls are fully cooked I transfer them to a big pot of simmering soup, so they will gently absorb the flavor of the soup, before serving.

Ingredients

- 4 eggs
- ½ cup seltzer
- ⅓ cup olive oil
- 1 cup matzo meal
- ½ teaspoon kosher salt
- ¼-pound leftover brisket, cut into ¼-inch cubes

Directions

1. In a medium mixing bowl beat eggs with a fork for 30 to 60 seconds.
2. Add seltzer and oil and beat together another 15 to 30 seconds.
3. Add matzo meal and salt and mix together until just combined, don't overmix.
4. Cover and place in the refrigerator for 30 minutes or until firm.

5. In a medium-sized pot, bring 3 quarts of well-salted water to a rolling boil. Reduce heat to a simmer.

6. Scoop out a heaping tablespoon of the matzo ball mixture and flatten it in your wet or well-oiled hand.

7. Place 4 to 6 brisket cubes in the middle and wrap the matzo ball around it. Gently roll in the palms of your hands to form a round smooth ball.

8. Carefully drop the matzo ball into the simmering salt water. Repeat with remaining ingredients.

9. Cover and cook for 30 to 40 minutes.

10. Cooled matzo balls can be refrigerated for a few days or frozen for a few months.

11. Before serving, add matzo balls to a pot of your favorite simmering soup and gently heat through. Ladle into bowls and serve warm.

Prepared shawarma spice is available ready-to-go from spice manufacturers, but if you want to make your own, simply combine:

1 Tbsp. ground cumin
1 Tbsp. ground coriander
1 Tbsp. toasted garlic powder
2 tsp. paprika
1 tsp. ground turmeric
1 tsp. ground black pepper
½ tsp. ground cloves
½ tsp. ground cayenne pepper
½ tsp. ground cinnamon
Pinch kosher salt

40 Best Brisket, Sides, Slaws and Leftover Recipes

Pulled Brisket Shawarma Pitas

1 hearty (stuffed) pita

I might be partial but Israeli street food is my absolute favorite. A soft, fresh, pillowy pita slathered with hummus and charif, stuffed with shawarma (or falafel), plus sides and salads like crunchy pickled veg, cabbage salad, fried eggplant, Israeli salad, spicy carrots, chopped Israeli salad, sumac dusted onions and fresh parsley - smothered in tahini and amba is the thing food dreams are made of. So it's quite easy to imagine how my favorite leftovers turned into my favorite street food.

Ingredients

1 tablespoon olive oil
1 cup shredded/pulled leftover brisket
1 teaspoon shawarma spice (see sidebar)
1 soft fresh pita

Favorite spreads and sauces like:
Hummus
Charif
Babaghanoush
Tahini
Amba

Favorite sides and salads like:
Chopped Israeli salad
Israeli cabbage salad
Coleslaw
Crunchy pickled veg
Moroccan salad
Turkish salad
Sumac dusted onions
Spicy Carrots
Fried eggplant
Fresh parsley
Pickles
Hot peppers (pickled or fried)
"Chips"/fries

Directions

1. Heat a sauté pan large enough to hold the brisket over medium high heat.

2. Add oil and shawarma spice to the hot pan. Toast for 30 seconds to cook and release the flavors of the spice blend.

3. Add brisket and sauté for about 1 minute more to coat in spices and to heat through.

4. Slit 1 pita at the top to create a large pocket. Spread on hummus, charif and or babaghanoush.

5. Stuff by layering brisket shawarma with your favorite sides and salads.

6. Top with a generous drizzle of tahini and or amba.

BBQ Brisket Sandwiches

4 big sandwiches

We have a few favorite restaurants, Hubby and I—none that we agree on, of course. When he wants steak and fries, I want blue cheese, pear, and arugula pizza, so I started making it for myself. He's a Chinese-right-out-of-the-carton, standing-up-at-the-counter kinda guy; I just love being waited on, love a beautifully set table, love fancy napkins and those waiters with white gloves. Makes me feel like a duchess dining at my magnificent ancestral estate. "That will be all, Charles."

But anyway, we do have one place in New York City that we both adore, and even one dish we order right away to split: their Pulled BBQ Short Rib Sandwich. Okay, to be honest, we usually order a main for each of us, plus the sandwich to share. (I can't believe I'm actually confessing this in print.) Since we crave this dish, I decided to try it at home. Good thing I don't frustrate easily. Not too easily, anyway. It took about 15 pounds of meat, but I finally, finally perfected my version of our fave sandwich.

When developing brisket leftover recipes I thought how fabulously perfectly braised pulled brisket would stand in for the short ribs. And I am SO happy to report that I was right!

Ingredients

- 4 sandwich rolls or hamburger buns
- 8 teaspoons olive oil
- Toasted garlic powder
- 4 cups shredded/pulled leftover brisket, warmed
- 4 tablespoons mayonnaise
- 2 tablespoons prepared red horseradish, or more to taste
- 4 tablespoons BBQ Sauce
- 2 medium avocados, pitted, peeled, and sliced
- ½ cup Crispy Shallots (recipe pg. 100)

Directions

1. Drizzle each bun with 1 teaspoon oil and a few dashes of garlic powder, then broil on high, cut side up, for a minute to toast.

2. In a small bowl whisk together mayo and horseradish. Slather one side of each bun with horseradish mayonnaise and the second side with BBQ sauce.

3. Stuff with 1 cup meat, one-quarter of the avocado slices and one-quarter of the Crispy Shallots.

4. Continue with the remaining ingredients.

5. Serve warm with any of my **Slaws** (pgs. 79-86) or **Baked Spicy Sweet Potato Fries** (pg. 66).

Recipe adapted from the JOY of KOSHER Cookbook **by Jamie Geller (William Morrow/HarperCollins 2013).** Order your copy now **for 199 more fast, fresh, family recipes.**

"Breakfast" Brisket Hash

4 servings

I really am crazy about breakfast for dinner. Back in the day, my mom used to take us to the diner around the corner, and she'd let us order Belgian waffles. For dinner. The waitress would look at us like we were holding the menu upside down, but who cares? So while potatoes and eggs may be considered "breakfast food," I say this recipe is certainly acceptable as dinner fare too. (Tell me I'm right.).

Ingredients

2 tablespoons olive oil

1 medium (8-ounce) sweet potato, peeled and cut into ½-inch cubes

1 medium (8-ounce) russet, Yukon gold or red skinned potato, peeled and cut into ½-inch cubes

Kosher salt

Freshly ground black pepper

1 medium red onion, sliced

1 medium red bell pepper, ribs and seeds removed, cut into ½-inch cubes

1 medium green bell pepper, ribs and seeds removed, cut into ½-inch cubes

2 cups (1-inch) cubed leftover brisket

1 teaspoon ground cumin

1 teaspoon paprika

Directions

1. Heat the olive oil in a large ovenproof skillet over medium-high heat.

2. Add the potatoes, season with salt and pepper and sauté until just starting to brown, about 10 minutes.

3. Add the onions and bell peppers (adding more oil if needed), season with salt and pepper and sauté until slightly softened, about 5 minutes.

4. Add the brisket, cumin and paprika; sauté 5 minutes more or until the veg is soft and the brisket is slightly crisp and heated through.

5. Check for seasoning.

6. Serve with fried eggs of your choice.

Stuffed Latkes

10 to 12 Latkes

The idea for stuffing latkes came from Shifra Klein, our Editorial Director. She came up with combos like Smoked Salmon and Green Goddess Dressing Stuffed Latkes, Apple and Cheddar Stuffed Latkes (pictured on p.119) and these Pulled Brisket and BBQ Sauce Stuffed Latkes. This combination tastes similar to a pulled beef sandwich; the ultimate latke for any meat and potato lover.

Note: Cornmeal will make your latkes extra crispy.

Ingredients

- 4 medium russet potatoes, about 2 pounds
- Canola oil or olive oil
- 2 eggs, beaten
- 2 tablespoons matzo meal or cornmeal
- 2 teaspoons kosher salt
- ½ teaspoon coarse black pepper
- 1 cup shredded/pulled leftover brisket mixed with ¼ cup BBQ sauce
- Applesauce, optional

Directions

1. Prepare a large bowl filled with cold water.

2. Peel potatoes, and as you finish each, place in cold water to prevent browning.

3. Heat ¼–inch of oil in a large skillet over medium heat.

4. Grate potatoes on the side of a box grater or cut potatoes lengthwise into halves or quarters so they fit into a food processor feed tube. Process potatoes using the blade that creates thin, shoestring-like strips.

5. Squeeze excess moisture from the potatoes, by hand (in fistfuls) and pat dry with paper towels or wring out in a kitchen towel until really dry (like really, really, really dry) and transfer to a large bowl.

6. Add eggs, matzo meal, salt and pepper and mix well.

7. Drop a heaping tablespoon of latke batter into hot oil. Using the back of a spoon, pat down the latke to flatten it.

8. Place 1 tablespoon of the shredded brisket and BBQ sauce mixture onto the latke.

9. Top with another heaping tablespoon of latke batter and pat down with the back of a spoon to flatten it and "sandwich" the brisket stuffing.

10. Fry 3 to 4 minutes on each side, until golden and crisp around the edges.

11. Repeat with remaining ingredients frying 2 to 3 stuffed latkes at a time, careful not to overcrowd the pan. Frying too many latkes at once will make them soggy.

12. Drain on paper towel lined baking sheets.

13. Serve warm with applesauce if desired.

| *40 Best Brisket, Sides, Slaws and Leftover Recipes*

Southwestern Brisket Frittata

8 wedges

Slice and serve wedges out of this hearty pretty frittata—just divine with a dollop of non-dairy sour cream and a touch of salsa.

Ingredients

2 tablespoons olive oil

2 large red potatoes, scrubbed and thinly sliced (about 1-pound)

1 small onion, peeled and thinly sliced

1 red bell pepper, thinly sliced

1 clove garlic, minced

10 large eggs

2 tablespoons plain soy or almond milk

½ teaspoon kosher salt

½ teaspoon freshly ground black pepper

½ cup shredded/pulled leftover brisket

½ non-dairy sour cream

1 cup salsa

Directions

1. Preheat oven to 400°F.

2. Heat oil over medium heat in a 12-inch, nonstick, ovenproof skillet.

3. Add potatoes and cook 10 minutes or until just tender.

4. Add onions and peppers, cook 5 minutes more, or until onions are translucent.

5. Add garlic and sauté until fragrant about 1 minute.

6. In a large bowl, beat eggs with non-dairy milk, salt and pepper.

7. Stir in brisket. Pour over potatoes and onions and transfer to preheated oven.

8. Bake at 400°F for 15 to 18 minutes or until set in the middle.

9. Loosen edges with a spatula and slide out onto a plate.

10. Cut into 8 wedges and serve with non-dairy sour cream and salsa.

Jamie Geller is the only best-selling cookbook author who wants to get you out of the kitchen—not because she doesn't love food—but because she has tons to do.

As "The Bride Who Knew Nothing", Jamie found her niche specializing in fast, fresh, family recipes. Now the "Queen of Kosher" (CBS) and the "Jewish Rachael Ray" (New York Times), she's the creative force behind JamieGeller.com

One of the most sought-after food and lifestyle personalities worldwide, Jamie is changing the face of traditional Jewish cuisine by putting a healthy, family-friendly spin on all the classics. She also shares the Modern Israeli way to cook. And she enjoys integrating this "new Mediterranean style" of meal planning and prep in everything she creates.

Jamie and her hubby live in Israel with their six super kids who give her plenty of reasons to get out of the kitchen—quickly. Check out her latest book, "JOY of KOSHER Fast, Fresh Family Recipes" and her new family meal plan "Fresh Families" at FreshFamilies.us.

Made in the USA
Lexington, KY
06 May 2018